T0120875

# I Love You MORE

For Mothers in Faith-Based
Treatment Battling Addiction

JEANNINE HARRIS

WESTBOW
PRESS®
A DIVISION OF THOMAS NELSON
& ZONDERVAN

WestBow Press books may be ordered through booksellers or by contacting:

WestBow Press
A Division of Thomas Nelson & Zondervan
1663 Liberty Drive
Bloomington, IN 47403
www.westbowpress.com
844-714-3454

ISBN: 978-1-6642-2509-1 (sc)
ISBN: 978-1-6642-2508-4 (e)

Print information available on the last page.

WestBow Press rev. date: 04/26/2021

# CONTENTS

*I dedicate this book to my daughter, Jillian Marie, my best girl. I thank my incredible family who never gave up on me and loved me through it all. The sacrifices they all made for me will never be forgotten.*

What you are about to read is not a feel-good book to excuse your poor choices, nor is it a pardon with great psychological jargon to justify why you did, what you did, that got you where you are. I'm sure at this point you do not need any more guilt and shame – so this is not intended to make you feel any worse than I know you feel. Here, in my recollection, is an offer of hope - a hope that brings with it the fact that no matter what has transpired, with an acceptance and responsibility of your present reality, you can believe this is not all there is. This is not the end of things, but a wonderful beginning if you allow time and process to have their way. More importantly, is that you allow God to have his way in your life. Have you had your fill of disappointment? Can you get any more discontented? Can you go any lower? Whether you believe or don't believe does not alter the fact that there is one true sovereign being that can do the impossible. That being is God and with a broken, contrite, surrendered heart dependent now on Him rather than self, He will show Himself mighty in your life. If you are like me, I would never have believed that my circumstances could change, but at that time I did not fully understand the power and providence of the Almighty God.

# INTRODUCTION

This is a book for and about mothers who have lost (physically, emotionally, legally, temporarily, permanently) their children due to addiction, or any other life-controlling issue. If you have not lost your children yet, I can assure you that if something does not radically change in your life, losing them will be inevitable. You are not the exception to the rule. You are not invincible. You are not smarter than the system. Your prowess, keen, slick street sense did not quite serve you in the end, did it? For here you are, and I know that you have been given an opportunity from this day forward to never have to go back to where you once came.

If you're wondering why you should read this book, and if you're doubting that your situation is reparable, here is a list of scenarios that will explain why you should. You/your:

- lost custody of your child/children
- have joint custody
- family is caring for your children
- children are custody of the state
- children were born addicted or with a disorder due to physical abuse
- drug abuse started or escalated due to the unrelated death of a child
- child's death was due to your addiction
- willingly gave your children up for adoption

- were forced to give your children up for adoption
- currently in a program that has given you the privilege of having your children with you

It is possible that I haven't covered every situation imaginable, but I am confident that I have listed those that many of you find yourself in - if not these exact situations, probably close to one, if not more than one. For most people suffering from a life-controlling issue, it always begins with one decision that sets it in motion, and it never gets better until it is eradicated, not just temporarily stopped. I stopped many times; in and out of detoxes and 28-day facilities. Successful completion of these programs just didn't have the permanency that I was longing for. I was promised that as my use continued and the addiction worsened, without any true healing, without any deep-heart transformation, I would begin to suffer more and more of these harrowing predicaments. I never wanted to believe it. I didn't believe it, nor did I understand it. I didn't have anything to base it on. After all, it was all new to me – in the beginning. But then, as I became a "seasoned" addict, a veteran to the insanity, destruction, and despair, I had to admit that everything I was told that would happen, did.

With great thought and careful consideration, I have laid out this book as practical as I could. My hardships and sufferings were not in vain. I know that when I was being helped by wonderful, well-meaning women, not all of them were mothers. It is my hope for you, as a mother, that you can relate to this book. I have taken incredible comfort and knowledge from so many amazing people, however, there is something so profoundly inherent within a mother's heart that only another mother can understand. It is my prayer that you will consider this while you are reading.

If you're anything like me, you may have tried many different ways to finally conquer your addiction, or at least push back the horrible consequences and get right for a while. If I was able to do that, then I could have assured all those around me that I was okay. Honestly, all my failed attempts were largely due to a lack of a genuine "want" to get well. Intuitively, I knew it. Sure I loved the feeling of being high – any altered state was better than being in my own skin. But let's not kid ourselves, ladies. We drink and do drugs because it feels good. Sin is pleasurable, but for a season. It is sin. The world would have you believe that you have a disease.

On the merry-go-round of physical and mental wellness, like me, you've probably tried 28-day programs, 3-month programs, detox units, inpatient programs, outpatient programs, holistic methods, vitamin supplements, meditation, anti-depressants, anxiety medications, physical exercise, and relationships, just to name a few.

Perhaps you haven't concluded yet that God needs to be in it. If you have participated in secular step programs, they unabashedly proclaim you must find God, and you must find Him now. So why would it be different if you hear the same suggestion within this program? I pray that while you're reading this you're at least determined to give God a try. You will not be disappointed. After all, you've tried everything else, right?

My concern is not whether or not you've shunned the "God thing" or if you have faith or believe in God, yet. What I do know for sure is that when we can wholeheartedly admit that on our own, we have failed to accomplish full and lasting healing, we're ready for permanent change. If you have asked yourself the question over and over, *How did my life get to this?* You're in a perfect position. I've often shared that there is great freedom in waving the white flag of surrender. When we ultimately come to the end of ourselves and admit, I'm done, I'm broken, I'VE TRIED, I CAN'T...THAT IS WHEN THE GREAT TRUTH IS REVEALED. BECAUSE YOU ARE CORRECT, YOU CAN'T. BUT, HE CAN.

*one*

# I AM SO AFRAID

I don't need to go into an academically precise definition of what fear is. We've all experienced it, we know it well and it is something that either stops us dead in our tracks or propels us to move forward despite it looming over us. Fear has its necessary function as it causes us to assess what is going on around us, who is around us, and what is the danger that may be imminent. We may then proceed with caution. This is not the fear I'm talking about. Here you are, in an environment where nothing at first is familiar. You are not in control of basically anything but to follow the rules set forth and be obedient to the people that have been placed over you. Your daily routine has been snatched away, and a day in the life of the program is not going to be anything like you are accustomed to. Now for those of you who were running on crazy, by yourself, (without having to currently care for your children) chances are you may be welcoming the normalcy that this program will give you. Rest assured, you know where your next meal will be. You will also have access to, and may even be required to shower daily (for some of you, sadly, that's an old-forgotten concept!!). That's all good, but you may find yourself thinking, *I'm a mom, I know how to multi-task. You don't know how hard it is to raise a child or several children. I did it all on my own.* Whatever your self-imposed claim to sanctified motherhood sounds like, somewhere deep within you is fear. It's okay. You don't have to admit it to everyone and if you've been through the legal system, you've probably developed a hard exterior to pretend you're tougher than you really are. Regardless, I believe some of these fears may sound something like, *I don't know what's going to be required of me? Are they going to make me do things I'm uncomfortable with? This program is too long, what if my children stop needing me? If I'm not out there to keep things together, "they" may try to take my children. What if I do this entire program and it doesn't work? How am I going to be here without having to do all the things that a mom does? After all, no one can do it better than I can.* These might be some of the thoughts that are provoking fear in you. I understand them well.

## PERSONAL ACCOUNT

When I walked through the doors of Adult & Teen Challenge, I was surprised at first. I had been to several other programs, but not a faith-based program. So, when I walked in and saw it was a home and not a state-run facility, I was pleasantly surprised and a little confused. I remember reading scriptures on the walls, I heard sweet singing somewhere in the distance, and I was asked by several women if I wanted to sit and eat dinner with them. I was afraid and cried for days. I didn't think I was going to get hurt, that wouldn't have mattered at that point, for I was already crushed in body, mind, and spirit. I was afraid I would never have joy again. To me, this was the end of everything I once knew to be "fun." Now it was time to pay the price and this was my punishment for living the way I had been. My life would never be worth anything and I was sure I'd never experience happiness again. It was all one big disaster. To top it off, my little girl was away from me. In my ignorance and cynicism too, I was sure that none of these women could understand what I was going through and they certainly hadn't experienced what I had. As I looked around and sized everyone up, I was sure of it, there was no one there who could come close to the pain I was in. Boy, was I wrong.

A while ago, I remember hearing that the flip side of fear is anger. Hmm? That was an interesting concept and as I let that settle in my mind, I had to admit there was truth in it. I was angry. I was angry that I was there, that I had become a drug addict, a scared, single mother who was misled, violated, disappointed, cast out from my family. I was angry that I was the once looked-up to oldest sister (maybe?) who was now the poster-child for "loser." I was angry that I was promised I'd be protected, and yet I was coaxed into a deplorable lifestyle. I was seething with anger that detectives had told my family what was going on in my personal life. The lies and all the painstaking work of hiding the ugly truth were exposed. Sure, I was furious. I was angry that no one saved me from myself and roiled at all those dysfunctional years of numbing the memories of my pedophile. I was angry that I spent countless hours in a therapist's office years before. I was a mess.

So many years of depression, anxiety, loneliness, searching for my identity, and there I was. There were countless desperate measures to fill my emptiness which only magnified my emptiness. There were bouts of exercise, holistic rituals, visits to ashrams, and still no remedy. I was a 45-year old woman sitting in a place called Adult & Teen Challenge. Everything I had accumulated was gone, including myself, and more importantly my child.

But, God.

# Two

# I HAVE RUINED EVERYTHING

This is an excerpt I found in my journal in 2010. At that time I did not know that this would be part of my book. I didn't even know I would be writing this book.

*A young woman said, "I love drugs. I absolutely love everything about them," said the teen being interviewed. "Whatever it takes to get them, I wouldn't think twice about doing it."*

*Most people would find that statement baffling, hard to*

*understand how anyone could say that – unless you were an addict. I was one of those people years ago who would shake my head at a statement like that. In my mind, I thought with a certain air of superiority "how do people get to that point? What a shame! Look at them! I just can't imagine why anyone would allow that to happen." Today, I not only understand it, but I am also one of those people. Now, I'm in a long-term residential facility, it's an MTARP (methadone abstinence residential program). At some point each day I wonder- how did I get here? I had a life filled with hopes and dreams and I'm surrounded by methadone zombies, being told where to go, what time to get up, and of course, staff and doctors dictating to me what dosage of methadone I should be on to satisfy my residency (and keep my bed) in the program. This is complete insanity. I'm not one of these people! I'm not!!*

Well, if you're wondering what happened, I did stay in that program for several months, but I was determined to get out and get my baby back. I had to finally get off methadone once and for all. The program would not budge and they were tapering me off very slowly. It would have taken months at the rate they were going. At this time my daughter was down in Virginia with my sister and I could not travel to see her because I had to go to the clinic daily to get my methadone. I wasn't having it anymore. I locked myself in a room that I rented in the Bronx, and during the blazing heat of July, for about one week I went cold turkey. I faced every nightmare physically, mentally, and spiritually. I'll spare you the details but if you have any idea what it's like to go cold turkey off opiates, I descended into hell. I've said this over and over again, "I wouldn't wish that on my worst enemy."

Fortunately, I did get off the methadone but left to my own devices without any accountability, I went back to the street for heroin. Yes, I did ruin everything again and again and again.

Fast forward about one year. I had moved home with mom,

kept using, crashed a car, threatened to jump off a bridge, got locked in a psych ward for 2 days, fought with Child Protective Services (CPS) caseworkers, went back to 12-step meetings…try and try again only to fail and fail over and over. Yes, I had ruined everything.

My paths crossed with someone in a step meeting who had been through the Adult & Teen Challenge program. At the very end of our friendship, he said he knew eventually I would wind up in the program. He was right. Eight months later, my family found me on the front lawn of my brother's house completely incoherent. It was Mother's Day. The phone calls were made and there was a bed waiting for me. Four days later I entered New York Adult & Teen Challenge, a long term, faith-based residential program.

I sat inside the Grace Home ashamed and full of self-loathing. I grappled with incomprehensible guilt, heartbroken, rejected, and dejected, but here I was trying something new, so desperate, yet hopeful. *How many times can one person fail? How many times can we promise and still mess up? How come I can't stop this addiction that is so cunning and powerful? Will I ever be free?*

It doesn't matter how we were raised, our educational background, with or without church, abused, privileged, abandoned, spoiled, ultimately, we share the same outcome, we became troubled addicts.

Things become ruined, but before something can be rebuilt and made new it obviously must be broken. It is meaningless to stay angry. You must keep a clear view of what you have become, followed by a determination to become who you were meant to be. It may be very hard right now for you to remotely understand any of this. There's an old saying, "If you want to know your past, look at your present conditions. If you want to know your future look into your present actions." What are your present actions?

Have you worked hard at your sobriety? Did you do everything in your power to undo all the wreckage you caused? I believe you may have. But one thing I know for sure is that staying stuck in the past and beating yourself up for all the shameful acts you've committed will only keep you stagnant. You need to be proactive and regain your life – a new life. This will not and cannot be in your own strength though. I hope by now you know that there's no denying this thing got the best of you, and it's going to require a greater strength.

## *Three*
# IT HURTS SO MUCH

The best way I can explain how I felt at that time, was completely and utterly crushed in spirit. I mean crushed!! Forget how my body ached and my mind was reeling. The very essence of my soul had no pulse, I was dead. I was disappointed and believed my life-long dreams were never going to be realized. As bad as that may be, the separation between my daughter and me could not compare. As I surveyed my surroundings, many young women were cackling and carrying on, almost giddy to the point of ad nauseam. I believed they had no idea of the pain I was experiencing. It is true, some did not because they were not mothers. It wasn't until later on that I befriended many other mothers and learned of their tragic stories. Compared to them, I actually could consider myself fortunate. My daughter was with family and she was still technically mine. That didn't matter then. There was a loss. I knew what it was like to hold my little girl tightly and have her taken from me. On one account, I was loading up my car, intoxicated, getting ready to put her in the car seat and drive. My youngest brother pulled up behind me and he took her from me. Begging him to let go and leave us alone, he won and he saved our lives. Had my sister not called him, I'm certain there would have been a devastating outcome. The screams swirling in my head became like an unceasing chant, *You're unfit, you're unworthy, you're undeserving.* I remember sobbing uncontrollably. Everything hurt, but most of all my heart was was so heavy. When I think back to that time, my eyes still well up. I was sinking deeper into a black hole and I couldn't climb out. I would have done anything for my little girl, and yet.

Yes, it hurt so much but here is a truth to comfort you, mom. If your child(ren) are with safe people, from a standpoint of children's wellness concerning parental separation - if a child benefits from highly loving, nurturing, positive relationships from other relatives/people, the child may not feel the effects of a mother figure's absence so greatly. As much as you may be obsessing over your separation, this is your obsession. Chances are, they are carrying on the way children naturally do. Of course, I am referring to younger children. I know it doesn't take away all of the pain, but if you could tuck that away in your mind and heart, I intend that you will get a touch of relief from your present pain.

Mothers, if that scenario is not yours, and it's not even remotely close, there is peace and there is solace for you too.

*Lord, ease my troubled mind and impose your virtue, your righteousness, and your comfort upon my aching body and mind. I may not know you or have faith in you, but please show yourself real to me. Please, Lord, give peace to my mind. If you are who you say you are, I give you every shed tear and beckon you, Lord, to help me get through this.*

The scripture that I held fast to during my whole program was Philippians 4:6-7 "Do not be anxious about anything, but in everything, by prayer and supplication with thanksgiving, let your requests be known to God. And the peace of God, which surpasses all understanding, will guard your hearts and minds in Christ Jesus."

His Word never failed me.

# *four*
# "BUT THEY NEED ME"
# - TRUTH VS. LIES
# WE BELIEVE

You are here, wherever that may be. Most likely, your children aren't with you. Unless you have been given a wonderful opportunity to have your young ones with you, they are somewhere else. This decision to change your life is the greatest one you will ever have made. But I tell you this from experience, unless you are completely, unconditionally sold out to stay this course, (no matter what happens and no matter what emotions may come your way), you will be on shaky ground.

Do you believe you are a failure? I know I did. What I came to find out was that I was **not** a failure, though I did fail. What made me realize I wasn't a failure was the fact that I made the radical choice to stay the course and pursue this unfamiliar territory. The word *radical* comes from the Latin radix "root" and finally I was determined to get to the root of the issues in my life, or for a better term, truly to the heart of the matter. Times will get tough, loneliness and longing will set in, there will be confusion as to why you chose this from the beginning, and so many other thoughts are going to flood your mind. These do not have to stay permanently. They can and will subside if you choose to accept them for what they are and stand up to them. Toughen up, you can do this! I haven't met a mother yet who hasn't had these thoughts while in treatment.

I started to convince myself that it wasn't fair for me to be taken care of while my daughter was out there. What a farce that was! Looking back now I can see how that was my pity party. If it wasn't for one of the staff members to tell me that if I continued thinking that way, I would walk out the door. But because I didn't, I'm able to be sitting here eight years later, writing this book, married to a pastor while my fifteen-year old daughter is at her Christian youth group. (I entered the program six days before her seventh birthday). This certainly wouldn't be the case if I believed the lie that "she needs me" and I left. Once you start thinking that you shouldn't be in a program because your children need you, let me assure you, you are in very dangerous waters. Two truths are going on. The first one is yes, they do need you, and the second one is that this thinking will take you out and quite possibly ruin a future with them. Because your children need you is the exact reason you should continue to fight steadfastly to remain planted where you are. Stop running, stop procrastinating, stop being selfish, stop doing what you always do, and relinquish control of your life to the people around you who will help you. Children need stability. Your addiction is making their lives unstable, regardless of how much you think you were there for them. Remember how you would take them to undesirable places, have them around strange people, used money that could've been spent on them? Yes, your children need you, but they certainly don't need that.

I have seen over and over mothers who believed they had to go home because their children needed them. More often than not, their circumstances did not improve, and sadly many of those mothers eventually died. Yes, their children did need them just like yours does. Those women permanently lost the chance to grow and mature into godly mothers – ones who nurture, encourage, provide, protect, train, coach, and discipline their children.

God is for you and He will give you the strength you need to battle these temptations that are determined to pull you back into the world. This truth is not only for those of you who still can be restored to your children. It is also for you as a woman, to be a light to every person you meet.

*five*

# WHAT IF THEY STOP LOVING ME?

Who do you love with all your mind, heart, soul, and strength? Before "children," people's first response to this question is usually their mom, the life-giver. That might not be your first answer, and it doesn't have to be. But I want you to think about how much you love your children and believe that they love you just as much. A mother's love shapes individuals, communities, and nations. It is a power that surpasses all circumstances. Fear, too, is a great impulse prompter. The thought of being pushed aside or forgotten can jounce us right out the door, running to coddle and fix all the wrong we've done; if we're even able to. We'd like to believe that our love is so strong for our children that nothing can stand in the way. Well, I think you know by now that may be true, but there will be forces that stand in the way: family members, friends, and the law. The only thing that would be detrimental is if you walk out on the place and program that you are in now. You will find yourself in no better shape, but the strategy to get you right back where you started will inevitably succeed. Don't lose your future to a present, pervading thought that your children will stop loving you.

I can't tell you for sure exactly what your children may be thinking about you and your absence. I don't know if you've been with them for a long time and this is a first-time occurrence for you being in a long-term program. Perhaps you haven't been and will not be in their lives anymore. I can confidently tell you that they may be very disappointed and angry at you and your decisions. I can guess that they might be confused as to why this keeps happening to you and them. One thing I've learned is that children don't stop loving their mothers because of their conditions. They just don't.

The phenomenon of children who have been abused and neglected by their parents and yet, still love them, is not hard to comprehend. The parent-child relationship is qualitatively more unique than any other relationship. It is endlessly fascinating. The bond between parent and child is one of the strongest connections in nature. Love is limitless and it knows no bounds.

## *six*

# I NEED HELP TO DO THIS – A NECESSARY SURRENDER

Hands up! Surrender! Wave the white flag. For some of us, these images invoke the fear noted earlier, legitimately defined as "an unpleasant emotion caused by the belief that someone or something is dangerous, likely to cause pain or a threat." *Surrender you say? You mean give up control over all things in my life? Give up my decisions, my habits, my thoughts, my way of doing things? Yes. It means that exactly. But it's the only way I feel in control.* I know. However, just because you feel like you are in control of these things doesn't necessarily mean you are. Our idea of control has been fortressed around a need to protect, to ward off violations, to ensure that nothing and no one is going to hurt you again. What an exhausting task to maintain over and over. This idea of being self-sufficient, independent, not needing any support from anyone is possibly due to numerous disappointments in your lifetime. The people who were supposed to protect you and provide for you failed you. They failed you miserably and so now it's up to you. *I got this* became your motto. If you had it all so together then why have you succumbed to a life dependent on substances and vices that have never supported you – never, never have they. Give up trying to control what is out of your control.

*Surrender you say? What does that even mean? And why is it necessary?*

You are in a fight, a relentless never-ending battle day and night. Hiding, maneuvering, sneaking, and deceiving have been your strategies. You've mastered them, or so you think and yet, you don't feel victorious. Guilt gets compounded, desperation has its claws deep in you, and you've constructed this impenetrable wall that you hide behind every day when you engage with the world. Day after day more and more of you shrinks until you're a shallow, hollow person who works tirelessly at having those around you believe you have it all together. You've lost yourself, but yet you're in control? Think about it.

It reminds me of my mom who refused to go into an assisted living facility because she didn't want to give up her home. She didn't want to give up her independence, and yet, each day she would wake, wait for her attendant to help her move into the living room and she would sit in her chair. From the bed to the chair was her substance of living. Occasionally there would be a doctor's appointment or a luncheon with her friends, but as for the day-to-day activities, that was it. Whereas, in the assisted living facility they have a daily agenda consisting of numerous activities: trivia, art classes, bus trips, educational lectures, movie night, etc. She had the opportunity to do all of this, but to have that she would have had to give up the control she clung to. The irony is, in her stubbornness, she believed she was living independently but truly she was dependent and limited. To have surrendered to the idea of going into the assisted living home, she felt she was losing something. Instead of relying on herself for this false independence, she would have needed to shift the dependence on the facility and their staff to offer her a better quality of life. Smug in her ways, prideful, frightened, she refused. She just couldn't surrender. As I continue to write this, just yesterday she moved in with me. There was much deliberation from family and friends as to what would be the best decision for her. Ultimately, she opted to not go to the assisted living facility, for now. In quiet moments, confronting her situation honestly and practically, she suggested temporarily moving in with me. Last night, her first night in her new bedroom, which may only be for six months or so, she went to bed with peace.

Yesterday, running around getting all things in order: seeing she had food, clean sheets, ample space for her clothes, toiletries, her walker and wheelchair, etc., she reminded me of me. I had become so dependent and broken and when I entered the doors of Adult & Teen Challenge I was in such need. I needed people to help me, to care for me, to make decisions for me. Truly, I had every need met and I was aided by a group of phenomenal women who understood my anguish. They were there to guide, comfort, and instruct me.

In the moment of full surrender, there is a transfer of power to those God has appointed over us. We succumb meekly. At the same time, God empowers us with His Holy Spirit to persevere and to endure. The transfer of wills goes from our sinful, prideful selves to the All-Loving, All-Forgiving, All-Gracious Lord whose will is perfect indeed. In His providence, if He does not give you something you want it is because He knows you do not need it. Though we may believe whatever we want will make us happy, His concern is not about our happiness but our holiness. Surrender your need for control and allow other, wiser, prayerful people to take the reins from your hands. Admit you are a woman in need.

*seven*

# HE WILL NEVER FAIL US

Lamentations 3:22 "The steadfast love of the Lord never ceases: his mercies never come to an end: they are new every morning; great is your faithfulness."

Imagine knowing someone unable to fail, unable to lie, who cannot forsake justice, and is faithful when we are not. Can you comprehend this? Can you grab hold of this truth as elusive as it may be in your own experience? Disappointment through broken promises or abandonment can cause deep-seated, scarred-over wounds that affect the way we see life. Our inter-personal relationships will most likely be strained because it's all we know. It's what we may have been exposed to most of our life. This broken heart has stolen your affection for life. Keep that in mind because trust comes easier to those whose trust hasn't been tampered with. I don't begin to doubt that every person, more than once, will in some way come face to face with a hope, a dream, or a desire and see it unfulfilled. Whether by our own choices, or by others who have avowed themselves to us, this display of trust not holding its end of the bargain disenchants us, and then a little more until we reach the point of ceasing to trust in anyone or anything. We may have not given up on believing we can trust ourselves. Right now, you can't and for that to be dismantled would mean it's either someone else we need to trust or absolutely no one. Undoubtedly, some persons hold the idea of trust with an open hand. This can be a very precarious place to live in, as skepticism will become the lens through which you view life. It eventually becomes a complete impossibility to trust anything unable to be seen or held. You must learn to trust. There's no way around this. Learn to trust.

Assuming you're willing to trust where you are and trust the success of your current program, it might help to understand what you are entrusting and to whom you are entrusting it. Is it your living conditions? Perhaps it is in helping restore a broken marriage through Godly counsel. You may need to get the law off your back and have all of your past and present charges disappear? The best answer, honestly, is all of it. A great idiom I remember hearing when I was seeking help was that there is only one thing that needed to change. For an instant, I got very excited. Awesome! I thought. Only one thing, fantastic! When I asked what that one thing is, the reply was EVERYTHING. It's not just one area in your life that needs changing. Please trust this to be true for yourself. Still obstinate, a know-it-all, and not yet admitting this openly, secretly I knew this to be true.

One of the first scriptures I had been given to memorize was Proverbs 3:5-6 "Trust in the Lord with all your heart, and do not lean on your own understanding. In all your ways acknowledge him, and he will make straight your paths." Why is that verse given? It's not because it's just short enough to memorize, or it sounds good. Within this scripture is the essence of taking our hands and our hearts off of our "stuff" and allow God to be God and straighten our paths. A straight path will get you where you need to be. A curved, rocky, distorted path will bring harm, delays, and diversions that bring us farther away from the desired end. Somehow, we have lost the ability to stay on that straight path, though we have determined so many times before to do so. Allow other people to help you help yourself. Let them redirect your steps and point you toward the path that is always available. It is never too late, and the damage is never irreparable when you fix your eyes on Jesus.

Paul makes it clear that he understood this well in Romans 7:15 "For I do not understand my own actions. For I do not do what I want, but I do the very thing I hate." God was intentional for he knew we all have this tension and conflict.

The straight path allows us to see what's up ahead, where we need to keep our eyes fixed rather than trying to find our way back on course over and over again. Off the straight path lies crevices and snares that tangle us up and prevent us from moving along the path of progress. We start with good intentions, but something happens along the way.

It's also important to consider the things that we want versus the things we need. If I'm truly trusting with all my heart, and not leaning on my understanding, then come what may, the surety of what the verse tells me that He Will make straight my paths has to happen. A familiar line in a secular song says, "You can't always get what you want, but you get what you need." *But why can't we get what we want?* You can and you will, but as I mentioned earlier, it might not come in the way you had hoped. It's crucial that you put the stake in the ground and commit, no matter what happens, I will trust when everything seems to be crumbling, or in your perspective, when nothing seems to be happening. Your circumstances may not seem to be changing at all, or perhaps they may seem to be changing for the worse. When you don't get the outcome you had wanted, you continue to trust. We can't make a demand for the healing to hurry up and fix all the past hurt. You see, as I had said earlier, imagine knowing someone unable to fail, unable to lie, cannot forsake justice, who is faithful when we are not. That is the Lord, the very One who has ordained for you to be in this program at this time of your life, in the middle of all the present struggles and consequences. It is He who commands you to trust in Him throughout this season of your life.

Psalm 118:8 tells us "It is better to take refuge in the Lord than to trust in man." Man will fail us, but by no means does this mean you should not trust the people that he has put in place over you. By doing that you are trusting Him because again, he is the one who will make straight your paths. He will use these individuals to accomplish His good will for your life.

If someone were to ask you whether or not you are trustworthy, how would you answer? Would it depend on what the situation is, or who it may be involving? Do you keep your word or someone's confidence? If you can say yes, then you understand the notion of what it means to be trustworthy. You may not have experienced much of it personally, but this is not a foreign concept. Think about the times in your life where you were not sure of what you were getting involved in, or for that matter, who you were getting involved with, but you jumped in head-first anyway. That is the mindset you will need to develop early on in the program, otherwise, your feet will not be planted deep enough and the surface roots that you are relying on will give way. We may work our fingers to the bones and our emotions into a ball of a knotted mess; all attempts to control our outcomes. But, the instant a personal storm blows in, or an external situation demands your attention, you will be swayed and uprooted. You need to trust deeply, trust wholeheartedly, trust with great expectation, trust through your fear. I can assure you that you have never been in a safer, healthier environment with endless possibilities. But without trusting God and how, when, and why he does what he does, you are resisting giving up control.

Hebrews 6:16-18 "For people swear by something greater than themselves, and in all their disputes an oath is final for confirmation. So when God desired to show more convincingly to the heirs of the promise, the unchangeable character of his purpose, he guaranteed it with an oath, so that by two unchangeable things, in which it is impossible for God to lie, we who have fled for refuge might have strong encouragement to hold fast to the hope set before us."

# eight

# HE IS THE GOD OF RESTORATION

Restored? What does it mean to be restored? Initially, I think of a piece of furniture that has been worn down, stripped of its shine, perhaps it has wobbly legs, crooked, and not steady. What's worse is that that piece gets to the place where it is no longer useful and it's not worth repairing. It met its end in the garbage dump. Or maybe you think of cars? houses? You get the picture. I know you have a good idea of what those look like, and probably have had experiences with them.

What about you? Will you continue to scrub and hammer away tirelessly without any difference made? Lord knows you had tried before. Not quite so shiny, huh? And still a little wobble in your leg? Sure. Many pieces make up the whole and you just can't seem to have them all working successfully, in unison. I know you can't because I couldn't. Then I lived my life in the faith and belief that God could. My feeble attempt at restoring myself to some wholeness was impossible. I needed no more reminding of that. I was limited, but what God could accomplish is limitless. And unlike that piece of furniture, no matter what condition we may arrive in, God will do more than repair us. His reparation is where ALL things are made new, not just improved. Revelation 21:5, "And he who is seated on the throne said, 'Behold, I am making all things new.' Also, he said, 'Write this down for these words are trustworthy and true.'"

Psalm 71:20 "You who have made me see many troubles and calamities will revive me again; from the depths of the earth you will bring me up again."

He is the God of Restoration. So, what exactly does this term mean? Well, there are several definitions for the word *restored*. There involves a renovation, restitution, and a return. To renovate is to remodel, improve upon the broken, damaged, or outdated structure. I don't know about you but "improved upon" sounds a bit too much like just getting a new wardrobe, maybe changing my hair, and making sure I look "remodeled" wherever I'm at. I'm not dismissing that our exterior probably could use a little more care and attention, but that hasn't gone far down enough for me. A surface change will give surface results. What we're after is something unlike anything before. A renovation renovates, but it doesn't always go deep into the foundation. Restitution is a reimbursement for a loss or injury or restoring to a former condition and then there's the returning to the former owner. He satisfied the longing soul, and the hungry one he will fill with good things.

Psalm 107:27-28 "They reeled and staggered like drunken men and were at their wits' end. Then they cried to the Lord in their trouble, and he delivered them from their distress." The Hebrew for "at their wits' end" is translated to mean "and all their wisdom was swallowed up." What a pitiful state to come to, all of our wisdom is swallowed up. It is gone, not present, not buried deep. Gone. What that tells me is that everything I think or attempt to do will not be guided by wisdom. How could it be that I have come to my wits' end and the only power that will restore me is a divine power that can do the impossible? Do you want to operate wisely? If yes, then stay right where you are, and you will have an encounter with that power. Your mind and your emotions will be restored.

1 Peter 5:10 "And after you have suffered a little while, the God of all grace, who has called you to his eternal glory in Christ, will himself restore, confirm, strengthen, and establish you." Wandering in the wastelands of ruin, wondering what happened to that compass of dreams you held fast to so long ago, you have become lost. Let yourself be returned to your former owner, the lover of your soul - whole and new.

During those times when the smokescreen of your thinking gets pulled back, and you start to experience the pains and sufferings of life and all the struggles, hopeless that anything can change, believe that God is able. He is a God of Restoration. It is in this divine refining, restoring process that God makes all things new and whole.

John 16:33 "I have said these things to you, that in me you may have peace. In the world, you will have tribulation. But take heart; I have overcome the world."

## nine

# HE ALONE IS OUR HEALER

Within the process of restoration, there will be healing, but before the healing takes place, it usually hurts some more. Hurt hurts a whole lot and nobody wants to hurt. We nurse wounds that fester into every area of our life. We go to sleep with them, and we rise with them. Heavy, hurtful, and haunting experiences continuously remind us of how imperfect we are and the world we live in. Not only are we imperfect, but so are our lives. Unless you feel, you will not heal. Remember that. Those uncomfortable areas in your life that you shrug off as not being that significant, or the ones you believe you've come to terms with, those are the ones that need deeper digging.

The power of rejection can stunt a person's emotional growth so pervasively to the point of paralysis. You become incapable of ever allowing yourself to become vulnerable. It's a deeply felt, personal assault when one is rejected. It whispers you weren't worthy then, and you're certainly not worthy now.

Along with rejection, there are abandonment issues incessantly fueling feelings of insecurity which linger and intrude on every relationship established. It feeds this unrealistic fear of being disconnected from someone or everyone. We wrestle with this gripping, governing fear that somehow, we may find ourselves alone living a life of insignificance. God knows this. Referring to the Israelites who suffered in captivity and were far from their native land, we have the promise given in Psalm 147:3 "He heals the brokenhearted and binds up their wounds." That promise is yours too.

Hurts have been hurled on to us, but we also have played our position. You cannot continue to make excuses because you've been hurt, abused, wronged, or left out. Not willing to confess and acknowledge your wrongdoing – the sins you have committed and admitting the ones that have been committed against you is crucial to your healing. You don't forget them by pushing them down, locking them up, and pretending they never happened. How have we hurt people? More importantly, how have we sinned against God? Unless you bring these egregious acts to the surface and expose them to light, you will not experience full and lasting healing. They will grow, nibble, gnaw, and then eventually devour you. As you're here in the program, you have a safe space and perfect opportunity to be healed from the bondage of evil, gross, perverted, distorted, disgusting sin which raged against you and that which you slung back. Develop healthy transparency. Turn yourself from the inside out.

The Bible gives a great description of how un-whole we are before God steps onto the scene: Psalm 38:3-8 "There is no soundness in my flesh because of your indignation; there is no health in my bones because of my sin. For my iniquities have gone over my head; like a heavy burden, they are too heavy for me. My wounds stink and fester because of my foolishness, I am utterly bowed down and prostrate; all the day I go about mourning. For my sides are filled with burning, and there is no soundness in my flesh. I am feeble and crushed; I groan because of the tumult of my heart." That was my condition nine years ago.

The woman who remains closed off and unwilling to become transparent is spiting herself. Her pain is just too great, the shame unbearable, and she just can't bear having others know about her past. Well, my friend, if that is you, then take a moment and ask yourself how beneficial has that been? If you believe that's not your problem, and you just need to stop being addicted and then carry on with life, you are sadly mistaken. Being open and honest should be your only option. It's time to get real and rely on the strength of the Lord to courageously and humbly confess. Ignoring those painful areas is like putting a salve over a wound with a tumor at its core. You will forever be applying a topical ointment, never getting to the cause. God wants to heal you. Your concerns are his concerns. God and his kingdom promises are established and for those who are in captivity, those with physical infirmities, He will heal them according to the measure of his grace. Again, He makes all things new.

I remember encountering two women in the program who hid their sin for fear of serious, maybe even legal consequences. They were closed-off and highly guarded. On the outside, they showed that things were getting much better, but it was so obvious that they were concealing some very disturbing experiences. They just wouldn't allow the light to shine on them. Both of these mothers left the program prematurely to carry on with life as they previously knew. Neither of these women were walking in victory. Both of these women loved their children deeply, and both had their children taken away from them. One has since died due to an overdose, and her children will never have the chance of reuniting with her ever again.

*Ten*

# THEY ARE HIS CHILDREN

As seriously as you love your children, as determined as you are to see them grow with health and happiness, to never want them to suffer or weep from pain, is as serious as God loves them too. Over and over in His Word, He speaks about children: how to teach them, not to provoke them to anger, how we should become like them. Children are important persons who will develop their unique personalities. A personality that will be a mosaic of ideas, opinions, convictions, rationalizations, and conclusions. Whether they are wee little ones, or grown adults navigating through this world and all its convoluted detours, they are resilient. You may have heard the phrase, "we don't give kids enough credit" when we come to find out how keen they are. We may later realize that all the off-kilter personalities that we brought home when we tried desperately to appear in our right mind, they always knew.

I don't know your thoughts on the mystery and wonder of how a child is conceived, and I know you don't remember being in the womb. You cannot because He made it that way. Perhaps you never thought about all the inner workings of conception. Science was never my strongest subject, but I can share with you that even God's Word acknowledges the marvels of his master design. Ecclesiastes 11:5 "As you do not know the way the spirit comes to the bones in the womb of a woman with child, so you do not know the work of God who makes everything." The child that came from you was from Him. In Psalm 139:13-16, the psalmist declares, "For you formed my inward parts; you knitted me together in my mother's womb. I praise you, for I am fearfully and wonderfully made. Wonderful are your works; my soul knows it very well. My frame was not hidden from you, when I was being made in secret, intricately woven in the depths of the earth. Your eyes saw my unformed substance; in your book were written, every one of them." Your children are his, he holds the original deed to their life, he just chose you to be the vessel that would conceive, carry, and give birth to that life.

Once you've committed to your program with an oath that you will finish what you started, remember that He is their father. Entrust their lives to his care. Pray for your children, for He has healing in store for them too. There are built-in features God knew to wire in children to protect them from the unpleasant, and at times very traumatic experiences they may become exposed to.

I'm not saying children won't remember painful events but within the framework of those experiences is a simple defense mechanism children rely on where they can deny or rationalize, even displace their emotional reactions onto substitutes. They can come out from underneath life's pressing weight. I've mentioned this to put you at ease. I know well enough that I desperately needed a way to believe my daughter would come out of this all, okay. I needed to believe that as I was seeing about the business of the Lord and His plan for my life, He would be faithful to see after her. If I didn't, my impulse to rush to make it all better would have thrust me right out the door on a mission that may have seemed very rational at the time. In reality, it would have just been another failed attempt to right all that was wrong, and the cycle would have repeated itself. In my imperfect ways to make something perfect, I would realize my inability, wallow in disgrace and give myself over to the destructive choices that brought me into the program in the first place.

I realize some of you may never get the chance to be with your children again. Whatever may be your circumstances, the reality is that you are a mother now, then, and forever. The moment that you conceived, or decided to become a mother through other means, maybe even adoption; that is when you took on the identity as a mother.

We, in our feeble, pretentious selves could never have conjugated the awesomeness of creating a life, had it not been for the Lord. Take a moment and let that comfort your troubled mind and heart. They are His, they belong to Him, and He will have His way. Make God the Absolute Father of their lives.

*eleven*

# IN HIS TIME

*Now! Why not now?!* The core of our being cries out for now! *If I could only have what I want now, you'll see; things will be different. I would be different; everything would be better.* Maybe I'm the only one who thought like this? I think not. We all know what it's like to long for, pine away for that person, that event, that acknowledgment. We want the party, the ring, the house, the happiness, the love, we want it now. We want the pain to go away, the family to be like it once was, the guy who slipped away from us to return, now. Now! Why can't it be now?! Why do we always have to wait? I admit, my patience needs a lot of work. Impatience and I have had a long relationship, and it's one that I need to sever. It never fails to remind me of how prideful I am, as if my timing is the one in which everything would be done properly and efficiently. I'd have a lot less discontentment if I would just remember God's timing is always perfect.

What's this idea of time anyway? As a youth time doesn't matter as much. Young thoughts don't go too far deeper than - I am here now. I live and at some point, in the future, I will be no more. That's the way I remember it. Not to say that younger people don't get impatient. But imagine if we could keep a log of all the events we rushed along. How many plans fell through because we forced them to happen? What about the people we were in too much of a hurry to give our time to? It is time that is so precious. There is no better time than the present. Tell yourself that you are ready for this now. Stop putting off until tomorrow that which you can accomplish today. Your time is now.

2 Corinthians 4:17-18 "For this light and momentary affliction is preparing for us an eternal weight of glory beyond all comparison, as we look not to the things that are seen but to the things that are unseen. For the things that are seen are transient, but the things that are unseen are eternal."

Ecclesiastes 3:1 "For everything, there is a season and a time for every matter under heaven."

Ecclesiastes 3:11 "He has made everything beautiful in its time. Also, He has put eternity into man's heart, yet so that he cannot find out what God has done from beginning to the end."

There is a time for everything, and this is the season in your life that has been carved out for you. You can't expedite healing. Stay the course, do the work, and not a minute of this time will be wasted. I promise.

*Twelve*

# NOW, WALK IT OUT

I hope by now you are convinced of your desperate need for something different; a need for critical, painstaking self-reflection. What this will require is a mature-minded, straight-backed, courageously determined woman who won't back down. Become that person who will permit people to point out your flaws and redirect your attention to constructive alternatives - not destructive ones. Accept the corruption in your heart and the self-serving agenda you have set for yourself. Acknowledge how out of sorts you are with your families and the absence of peace that has come about from these broken relationships. Allow the trajectory of your life to be recalculated, driven by the Spirit. Have you an absence of joy in your life? If so, you need to cut out the old ways of doing things, the hidden motives, the tucked-away secrets, and the sin that so easily entangles you. Joy will be yours, complete, and available every day. A full commitment to this program will be the springboard that catapults you into your new destiny. Old reactions to a conflict will be developed into new and improved ones. It won't happen overnight, and it won't happen in two or three weeks. Jesus' approach and response to what was being asked of him was obedience. He did not retaliate, nor did he avoid. Forget what you knew and invite a new way of thinking and doing. Breaking bad patterns of behavior will take time to cultivate. Past guilt, grudges, and failures have been so deeply embedded in how you see yourself, it will take time to not be affected by them. Unfortunately, the people involved in your life may never be able to let those hurts go. That will be their struggle, not yours. Don't shun them because they don't quite get what's going on with you. Unless they walk in your shoes throughout this program, they may not ever fully understand your transformation, but they will see it. It is not superstition, it is not magical, it is the living, breathing power of the Spirit of God that will bring your dead bones to life. You may not even realize it at first, but you will. When you start to implement the tools and truths of God's Word, it will be recognizable to those around you. They probably won't even know how to respond, but how you respond to conflicts will no longer be careless, but careful. You will develop discernment and discretion in word and deed. As you begin to walk out the full counsel of the Lord, a new you will emerge, one that will not be familiar to many who know you. You no longer have to try and become the person that others have deemed you should be. God will fortify you with his loving kindness and his prompting. Don't force it and don't fake it. Develop more and more, day by day. Walking in Kingdom character will show Jesus to others. Seek God and you will find His will along the pathway toward Him.

If you want the same consequences in your life, then keep on doing what you used to do. If you want to step off of the road to destruction and onto the narrow path that brings life, then stick it out and stay.

During my program, I encountered many battles. Family members were skeptical, and some were not ready to accept me. Others could not understand what kind of program I was in. Proclaiming Jesus at the center of my life was rather novel and though my family believes in Jesus, professing Him openly appeared overly zealous. This presented resistance and I learned early on that people will not be as excited as you are when you've met Jesus. I had to stand firm and not let that dissuade me. I wanted to please my family, I still do, and I wanted desperately for them to uphold what I had accomplished and what I was planning for the future. That didn't come easy, either. Though they were at ease about me being safe and no longer addicted, I still had much to prove. After finishing my program, it seemed practical to them that I should go and start taking the steps to get a job, maintain my sobriety, and start from scratch. I was even given an ultimatum that if I didn't leave after some time and get my life "going", without anyone's help, they would have to consider if/when I would get my daughter back. Supposedly, being able to do this all on my own would have justified that I was now better. True, but they were still apprehensive and had reason to be concerned. I see now that I couldn't expect an immediate new slate of forgiveness and trust from my family who had been so crushed by my addiction. Still, I persevered.

I had no home of my own to go to once I finished the program, and my daughter was still being raised by my brother and his wife. She was another daughter to them. My past work experience was all in the corporate world in New York City. That was just no longer an option for me. It became evident to me that I found my purpose and calling within the walls of the Adult & Teen Challenge program.

Within the twelve months of my program, I must have gone to over ten court appearances to try and get full custody of my daughter. There were times I was frightened, furious, and fragile. It wasn't a seamless process. I cried, I fought, but I never gave up.

In God's great providence, He had the best plan for my life. I decided to stay with the program for another year as an intern. The incredible leadership discipled me, trained me, and prayed for me. Within the year of my internship, I was given the opportunity to help pioneer a new women's home, the Hannah House, in Alcove, New York. The court was also astonished by the complete change in my living circumstances and my daughter Jillian was restored to me with full custody. I met my wonderful husband, Victor, who currently serves at Albany Adult & Teen Challenge. Together, we live a wonderful life with all of its complications, joys, disappointments, and bountiful celebrations. Whatever season we may be in, we are always ministering the good news of the gospel of Jesus Christ. I am forever grateful that I saw my program to completion, and you have no idea about the wondrous blessings that will flow into the lives of you, your children, your family, and your friends. When people witness your new life, it will be undeniable that you have been with Jesus. In my flesh, I am still not perfect, but I pick up my cross daily and forge ahead. " I have been crucified with Christ. It is no longer I who live, but

Christ who lives in me. And the life I now live in the flesh I live by faith in the Son of God, who loved me and gave himself for me." Galatians 2: 20-21

This is my story. You have a different story and a perfect one. If you allow God to make and mold you into the woman he intended you to be, your life will never be the same.

God bless you.

Printed in the United States
by Baker & Taylor Publisher Services